Creative Groups Guide

Dream Intruders

6
Complete Lessons

Adapted for Group Study by Tim Sutherland

STANDARD PUBLISHING
Cincinnati, Ohio

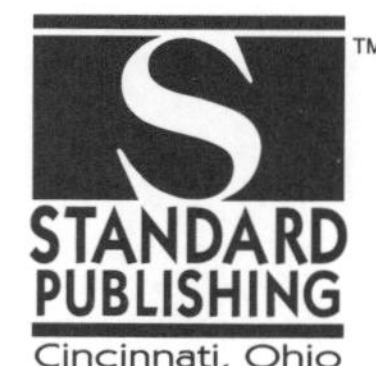

Creative Groups Guide: Dream Intruders

All Scripture quotations, unless otherwise indicated, are taken from the *HOLY BIBLE, NEW INTERNATIONAL VERSION*®. NIV®. Copyright © 1973, 1978, 1984 by International Bible Society. Used by permission of Zondervan Publishing House. All rights reserved.

Cover design by Listenberger Design Associates.

The Standard Publishing Company, Cincinnati, Ohio.
A division of Standex International Corporation.

©1995 by The Standard Publishing Company.
All rights reserved.
Printed in the United States of America.

02 01 00 99 98 97 96 95 5 4 3 2 1

ISBN 0-7847-0392-2

Contents

Foreword

I don't like dream intruders. I don't like to admit that life will never be exactly as I had dreamed and hoped it would be. A dream intruder is more than a temporary setback. It is an alteration of the planned course; a change of destination.

It would be nice if all of life were cloud-nine, a bowl of cherries, a walk in the park—but the real world is not like that. Accidents, terminal illness, being fired from a job, prodigal children, bankruptcy, and divorce weren't part of anybody's dreams. These intruders were not part of our plans.

Dream Intruders was written to reassure those of us who are meeting these intruders that we're not at the end. In fact, I'm learning that, when we feel as if we're at the end, that's often the point God is saying, "Finally, I've got your attention. I can do some of my best work in you right now." True life and true living begin only when our dream intruders bring death to our dreams and birth to the dreams that God has for us.

One of the difficult questions about dream intruders that is not capable of being answered in this guide is why they come. When dream intruders come, we seize reason by the throat and demand answers to our questions: Why me? Why now? When answers don't come instantly, like a pack of gum from a vending machine, we are further perplexed.

I offer this observation: you will probably not understand the *whys* of most dream intruders for a long time. So rather than offer *whys,* we will deal more with *what* and *how.* What do I do when a dream intruder comes? How do I get through it? May we hear the voice of God say to us as he said to Paul, "My grace is sufficient for you, for my power is made perfect in weakness" (2 Corinthians 12:9).

—Gene Appel, adapted from *Dream Intruders*

Introduction

Welcome to Creative Groups Guides!

Whether your group meets in a classroom at the church building or in the family room in someone's home, this guide will help you get the most out of your session.

You can use this Creative Groups Guide with or without *Dream Intruders,* the companion book written by Gene Appel. Use this guide even if you haven't read that book. But if you do read it, you'll be even more equipped for leading the group.

Each section in this guide includes two plans—one for classes and one for small groups. This gives the leader several options:

- Use the plan just as it is written. If you teach an adult Sunday school or an elective class, use Plan One. If you lead a small group, use Plan Two.
- Perhaps you teach a Sunday school class that prefers a small group style of teaching. Use the discussion questions and activities in Plan Two, but don't overlook the great ideas presented in Plan One. Mix and match the two plans to suit your class.
- Use the best of both plans. Perhaps you could start off your class with a discussion activity in Plan Two, and then use the Bible-study section in Plan One. Use the accountability or memory verse options presented in Plan Two in your Sunday school class. Use some of the "Sunday school" activities and resource sheets presented in Plan One in your small group meeting. Variety is the spice of life!

Resource sheets in each session are available for you to tear out and photocopy for your class or group. Overhead transparency masters are also included for some sessions. Use your own creativity as you decide how to make these resources work for you.

This guide has been developed to help you do several things. First, you'll be able to ***facilitate active and interactive learning.*** These methods help students remember and put into practice what they learn. Second, you'll ***help your class or group apply the lessons to their lives.*** These sessions will help your group members actually do something with what they're studying. Third, we've given you ***lots of options.*** Only you know what will work best in your class or group. Finally, ***support and encouragement*** are integrated into each session. Learning and application happen best when participants are helping one another. That may mean accountability if your group has built up the trust and caring it takes, or it may simply mean that people are lovingly encouraging one another to continue growing in knowledge and action.

How to Use This Guide

Each session begins with an excerpt from *Dream Intruders.* This excerpt summarizes the session at a glance. Use it in your preparation or read it to your class or group as an introduction to a session. The central theme and lesson aims help you understand the main ideas being presented and what outcomes you are looking for.

Materials you might need on hand to conduct your session are listed on the first page of each of the plans.

In both plans, there are three main parts to each session: *Building Community,* a warm-up activity or icebreaker question; *Considering Scripture,* Bible-study activities and discussion; and *Reflecting and Responding,* activities or discussion that will help participants apply what they have learned.

In Plan One for classes, the names of activities are listed in the margins, along with the suggested time for each one. Use these as you plan your lesson and as you teach to stay on track. In most cases, optional activities are listed. Use these instead of or in addition to other activities as time allows.

A number of options are included in Plan Two for groups. Use the accountability-partner option to help the group support, encourage, and hold one another accountable. This works particularly well in a group in which trust has already been gained among participants. Accountability partners can help one another put what they are learning each week into practice. An optional memory verse is also included. Use it at your discretion to help your group grow in hiding God's Word in their hearts.

Use this guide to help you prepare, but we suggest that you do not take this book to your class or group meeting and merely read from it. Instead, take notes on a separate sheet of paper and use that as you lead your group.

As you lead your class or group through these six sessions, remember that you are not trying to lead a recovery group or practice psychology. Be prepared for the possibility of deep emotions coming out sometime during this series; you'll be dealing with difficult issues that perhaps some participants have faced or are facing. Support, encouragement, and care for each other in the group are desirable, but group members should remember not to try to fix one another or counsel each other. Remember the words of Gene Appel: "God wants his family to be a community of 'wounded healers.' We help each other to rebuild broken lives and recover from dream intruders by the grace that we ourselves have received."

Dream Intruder #1

The Intruder of **Accidents**

Accidents happen. I know this doesn't make accidents any easier to deal with, but we might as well accept the fact that accidents will happen in our lives. That doesn't take the pain out, and I'm not suggesting we casually blow them off just saying, "Well, that's life. Qué será será." But the fact still stands—accidents happen.

We all know accidents happen, but we wonder why they happen to "good" people. I know people who say, "God must be getting me for something. There must be something bad in my life or this wouldn't have happened." Well, we've all got some bad things in our lives. Jesus taught in Matthew 5:45 that the sun rises on the evil and the good, and the rain falls on the righteous and unrighteous. In other words, accidents are no respecter of persons. We are talking about accidents: unforeseen, undesigned mishaps.

Anybody can be a Christian when things are going great, when all our prayers are being answered the way we asked them, when we're in good health, when our income is rising. The test of our faith is when problems come—when accidents hit. Accidents provide an opportunity for personal growth that probably would never occur in any other way.

—Adapted from *Dream Intruders,* by Gene Appel

Central Theme Accidents happen, and though we can't always stop them, we can prepare for them and grow through them because of our relationship with God.

Lesson Aim Students will become familiar with biblical examples of the fact that sometimes accidents do happen, learn how Paul dealt with a major accident in his life, and commit themselves to dealing with accidents by relying on God like Paul did.

Bible Background 2 Samuel 18:9–15; Luke 13:4; Acts 20:7–11; and Acts 27:14–44

For Further Study Read Dream Intruder #1, "Accidents," in *Dream Intruders.*

Plan One 

Classes

Building Community

Anxiety Index
5–10 Minutes

To introduce the series, begin class by distributing copies of Resource Sheet 1A, "Dream Intruders Anxiety Index." Direct students' attention to the quote at the top of the sheet and read it out loud. Instruct students to **Take a few minutes to complete the index on your own, marking how often you worry about each of the dream intruders happening to you or someone close to you.** After everyone has had a chance to do this, ask the class to divide into groups of three or four. In the groups, ask each person to **Briefly share two things: which dream intruder worries you the least (and why) and which one worries you the most.** (If your class is smaller, have students divide into groups of two or three or have individuals talk to the person sitting next to him or her.)

Option
Introduction
5–10 Minutes

Display the following quote on the chalkboard, a poster, or an overhead transparency to let people know what the new series is about:

> A dream intruder is more than a temporary setback. It is an alteration of the planned course, a change of destination. I don't like dream intruders. I don't like to admit that life will never be exactly as I had dreamed and hoped it would be.
>
> —Gene Appel, *Dream Intruders*

If the class doesn't already know what the topic of each lesson will be, ask, **What comes to your mind when you hear or read these words?** Then introduce today's topic by saying, **Tell the person sitting next to you about the first auto accident you were involved in: how old you were, where you lived at the time, who was driving, and other details.**

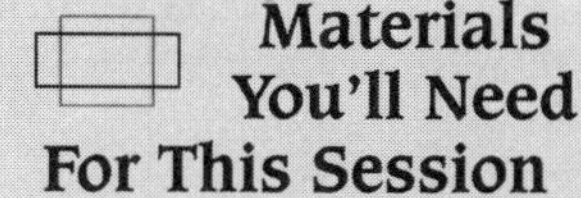

Materials You'll Need For This Session

Copies of Resource Sheets 1A-C; pens or pencils; poster board or butcher paper; and crayons, markers, or paints

Considering Scripture

Accident Report
5–10 Minutes

Distribute copies of Resource Sheet 1B, "Accident Report," and divide the class into three groups of six to ten. Then assign one of the passages of Scripture to each group for them to report on. (If dividing this way yields more than three groups, you can assign the same Scripture to more than one group.) Appoint a leader in each group to facilitate completing the sheet. After all the groups have finished, ask someone from each group to give the group's accident report to the rest of the class.

OPTION
Accidents Illustrated
5–15 Minutes

Divide into at least three groups. Assign each group one of these Scripture passages to read: ***2 Samuel 18:9–15; Luke 13:4; Acts 20:7–11.*** Direct each group to draw a mural, poster, or large cartoon of one of these scriptural accidents using butcher paper or poster board and markers, crayons, or paints. When all of the groups have finished, have them hang their poster, mural, or cartoon on the wall. Then have someone from each group tell about the accident they depicted.

Dramatic Scripture Reading
5 Minutes

Summarize the first Bible learning activity, and make a transition into the next activity by telling the class, **We see from these reports of accidents in the Bible that accidents do happen. Let's look at *Acts 27:14–44* to see how the apostle Paul dealt with a serious accident he was involved in.** (Explain that the writer of this passage is Luke, who traveled with Paul, so the students will not be confused by the use of the word "we" in that narrative.) Then pass out copies of Resource Sheet 1C and tell the students to notice as you read how the sailors aboard the ship reacted to the crisis and how Paul reacted. (Since this is a long passage, familiarize yourself with it in advance and read it with the kind of intonation and change of pace you might use if you were reading a story to a child for the first time.)

Bible Discussion
10–15 Minutes

After reading the passage, lead a discussion on how the students would characterize the sailors' reactions and Paul's reactions to the crisis. Keep the following ideas from the *Dream Intruders* handbook in mind as you lead the discussion.

The Sailors' Reactions

• First, they quit trying to sail and just allowed the ship to drift. Sometimes when a crisis hits, we think the best thing to do is just to let the circumstances carry us wherever we end up. The important thing is just to survive!

• Next, the sailors started throwing overboard everything they could get their hands on. In a crisis, we realize that some of the things we had thought were important are not so important after all.

• After all their valiant efforts to handle things on their own, they gave up all hope of being saved. They had forgotten God was in control, even in a crisis.

Paul's Reactions

• First, Paul planted himself on the rock. Paul stood on the rock of the Lord and said, "Keep your courage, men, I've got faith."

• Second, he remembered God was with him. In the midst of the storm, Paul said, "Last night an angel of the God whose I am and whom I serve stood beside me" (v. 23).

• Third, Paul relied on the promises of God. Paul told the men, "So keep up your courage, men, for I have faith in God that it will happen just as he told me" (v. 25). Paul believed and remembered the promises of God.

Reflecting and Responding

Personal Testimonies
10 Minutes

After discussing how Paul responded out of his relationship with God, ask individuals to share how God got them through serious accidents that came into their lives.

Prayer
10 Minutes

Close in a prayer time focusing specifically on two things: (1) preparing ourselves to respond as Paul did to any accidents that may come our way in the future; (2) praying for people the students know who are currently trying to cope with serious accidents in their lives.

PLAN TWO

Groups

PREMEETING

Cut out the three passages of Scripture from Resource Sheet 1B and pass them out to three people in the group as they arrive. (Be sure the three people you ask are comfortable reading aloud.) Tell them they'll be asked to read what you gave them later in the meeting.

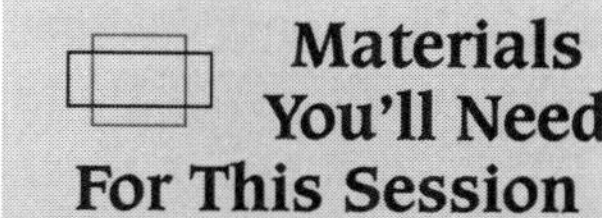

Materials You'll Need For This Session

Copies of Resource Sheets 1B, 1C, and 1D; and pens or pencils

BUILDING COMMUNITY

In groups of two or three, have each person tell about the first auto accident he or she was involved in: how old they were, where they lived at the time, who was driving, and other details. (If the group is small or just getting started, you can do this without dividing and ask volunteers to answer the question.)

CONSIDERING SCRIPTURE

• Move into the Scripture by saying, **There are many kinds of accidents that can happen to a person. Let's listen to some examples of accidents that happened to people in the Bible.** Then have the designated people read their passages of Scripture.

• Divide into units of no more than four, and hand out copies of Resource Sheet 1C. Explain that you are now going to explore an accident that happened to the apostle Paul and the people traveling with him. Tell each unit to select one person to read ***Acts 27:14–44*** aloud. (Or have one person in the whole group read the passage before breaking into the smaller units.) The rest of the unit should listen and take notes on their resource sheets as the passage is read. Appoint a facilitator in each group to lead a discussion about the differences between how the sailors and Paul reacted to the situation. Tell the groups how much time they have to complete the exercise.

• After the groups have finished, bring them all back together and lead a discussion of Acts 27:14–44. Use the notes in the Classes section of this session (pp. 10, 11) under "Bible Discussion" to guide your discussion. Depending on how much time you have, choose from among the following questions.

Option

Accountability Partners

Ask group members to pair up with one other person from the group to meet with or talk on the telephone with throughout this lesson series. For this week, ask them to discuss question three from Resource Sheet 1D, "Accidents and Me," about what they think would help them the most if a serious accident came into their lives.

Option

Memory Verse

"Your Father . . . causes his sun to rise on the evil and the good, and sends rain on the righteous and the unrighteous" (Matthew 5:45).

1. If you were one of the sailors and heard Paul say an angel told him everything was going to be fine, what would your reaction have been?

2. In verse 31, Paul told the centurion and soldiers that unless the sailors stayed with the ship, they wouldn't survive. Why do you think they listened to Paul and got rid of the lifeboat? What convinced them that he, a lowly prisoner, was worth listening to?

3. In verse 43, the centurion prevented his men from killing Paul. What do you think convinced him that Paul was worth saving?

4. Paul was visited by an angel with a promise from God to base his faith on during the crisis. Since we usually don't get visits from angels, what can we base our faith on in times of crisis so that we can keep our courage and trust God?

5. Which of Paul's words or actions would you find most encouraging if you had been on board the ship?

6. Verse 20 says, "We finally gave up all hope of being saved." Since Luke is the writer and he was a Christian, why do you think he gave up hope and Paul didn't?

7. Why do you think the sailors were encouraged after Paul gave thanks and ate in front of them in verses 34–36?

8. What would you have said to Paul when everyone reached land safely at the end of the crisis?

Reflecting and Responding

1. Direct participants to get back into the groups they were in earlier. Have them answer the questions on Resource Sheet 1D. Appoint a leader in each group.

2. Have each group close in prayer, focusing specifically on the fear of accidents and being prepared to respond to them with faith in God. Pray for anyone who is trying to recover from a serious accident.

Dream Intruder

ANXIETY INDEX

"I don't like dream intruders. I don't like to admit that life will never be exactly as I had dreamed and hoped it would be. A dream intruder is more than a temporary setback. It is an alteration of the planned course; a change of destination."

—*Gene Appel,* Dream Intruders

DIRECTIONS: Shade in the vertical bar up to the number that marks how often each of these dream intruders enters your mind.

High Anxiety

Very Frequently

Frequently

Fairly Frequently

Occasionally

Rarely

Never

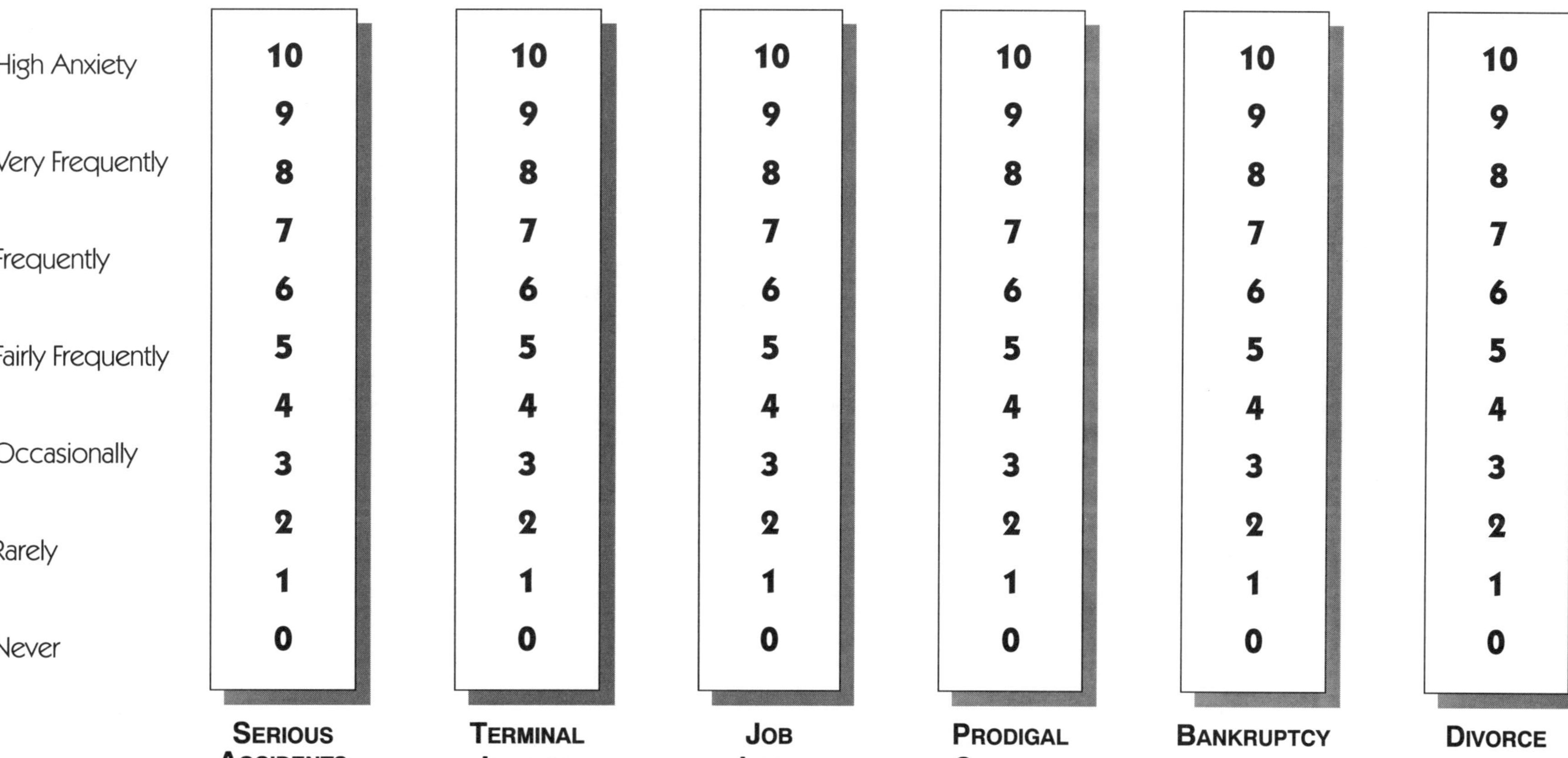

Copyright © 1995, The Standard Publishing Company. Permission to reproduce for ministry purposes only.

Accident Report

Read the account assigned to your group about an accident that happened in the Bible. Then answer the questions that follow and be prepared to give a report to the rest of the class. Write a one-paragraph newspaper story, including an eye-catching headline in the space provided at the bottom of the sheet.

2 Samuel 18:9–14
"Now Absalom happened to meet David's men. He was riding his mule, and as the mule went under the thick branches of a large oak, Absalom's head got caught in the tree. He was left hanging in midair, while the mule he was riding kept on going. When one of the men saw this, he told Joab, 'I just saw Absalom hanging in an oak tree.' . . . So he [Joab] took three javelins in his hand and plunged them into Absalom's heart while Absalom was still alive in the oak tree."

Luke 13:4
Jesus said, "Those eighteen who died when the tower of Siloam fell on them—do you think they were more guilty than all the others living in Jerusalem? I tell you, no!"

Acts 20:7–11
"On the first day of the week we came together to break bread. Paul spoke to the people and, because he intended to leave the next day, kept on talking until midnight. There were many lamps in the upstairs room where we were meeting. Seated in a window was a young man named Eutychus, who was sinking into a deep sleep as Paul talked on and on. When he was sound asleep, he fell to the ground from the third story and was picked up dead. Paul went down, threw himself on the young man and put his arms around him. 'Don't be alarmed,' he said. 'He's alive!'"

- What was the accident?
- How did it happen?
- Who did it happen to?
- Why did it happen? Who was at fault?
- What was the outcome of the accident?

Copyright © 1995, The Standard Publishing Company. Permission to reproduce for ministry purposes only.

Shipwrecked!

Acts 27:14–44

As the Scripture is being read, notice how Paul responded to the crisis and how the sailors responded. Make some notes to yourself in the space provided.

What the Sailors Did	What Paul Did

Copyright © 1995, The Standard Publishing Company. Permission to reproduce for ministry purposes only.

Accidents and Me

1. Have you ever had a serious accident happen to you that significantly changed your life?

- If yes, how did you deal with it?
- If no, what was the closest you ever came to a tragic accident?

2. At this point in your life, what effect do you think it would have on your relationship with God if a serious accident happened to you or to someone you love?

a. It would bring *doubts;* I would probably question whether God really cared about me.
b. It would be a *test;* I'd find out how much I really believe what I think I do about God.
c. It would probably *strengthen* my relationship with God; I usually draw closer to him in a crisis.
d. I would have no idea until it happens.
e. Something else: ________________________________

3. Which of the following principles would help you the most if an accident like the ones we've been talking about happened to you or to someone you loved?

a. No matter how bad it is, Heaven is the only permanent situation for Christians.
b. God's love for me can get me through any crisis that comes my way.
c. Accidents do happen, and someone isn't always to blame, including God.
d. Personal growth always comes with suffering when you're open to God.
e. God cares how I feel and wants to comfort me.
f. God has given me Christian friends to support me all the way.
g. I don't think anything would really help.

Copyright © 1995, The Standard Publishing Company. Permission to reproduce for ministry purposes only.

Dream Intruder #2

The Intruder of
Terminal Illness

No matter how many times I've been with families through the dream intruder of a terminal illness, through the long days of sickness, through the praying beside a hospital bed, through the cries of hopelessness wondering whether God is hearing their cries for help, this is one area of my ministry that I never get used to.

Not only does the patient suffer, but the family experiences incredible pain, anguish, and pressure. Those who are being left behind in a sense become patients themselves. Every day they live with the reminder that life will never again be as it was.

The reality that few of us like to admit is that we're all terminally ill. If nothing else, old age is a disease that will eventually take all of us. One of the best things all of us can do is to admit our own mortality—we are going to die.

When Jesus demonstrated his power over death by raising Lazarus from the dead, he also demonstrated that he has the power to raise you and he has the power to raise your loved ones. The key is faith in Jesus Christ. An ongoing relationship with Jesus Christ prepares people at any time for an untimely death.

—Adapted from *Dream Intruders,* by Gene Appel

Central Theme We need to be ready to minister as Jesus did to people experiencing the pain of terminal illness, and we also need be ready to face an illness that will end in our death.

Lesson Aim Students will learn and discuss biblical ways of helping people experiencing terminal illness, reflect on the inevitability of death for everyone (including themselves) and the Christian's victory over death through Christ.

Bible Background John 11:1–44; 1 Thessalonians 4:13–18

For Further Study Read Dream Intruder #2, "Terminal Illness," in *Dream Intruders*.

Plan One

Classes

Building Community

If It Happened to Me
8–10 Minutes

Follow the directions on Resource Sheet 2A, "If It Happened To Me," and divide the class into groups of four or five. Make sure you have enough sets of scenarios ready in boxes or bags to accommodate the largest possible attendance. Briefly explain the exercise before beginning: **Today's topic is a difficult one, so to get us thinking about it, we're going to put ourselves in the place of people who have had a terminal illness come into their lives.**

Let the groups know the time allotted for this activity; each person has about two to three minutes to respond to the scenario he or she draws out.

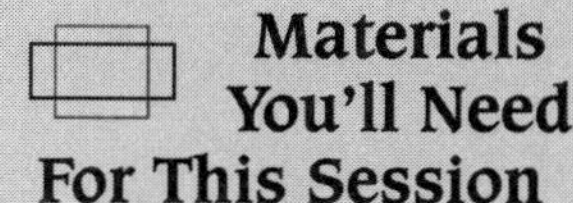

Materials You'll Need For This Session

Resource Sheets 2A–C, and small boxes or bags

Option
Gut-Level Reaction
5–7 Minutes

On the chalkboard or overhead write the following quote from *Dream Intruders*:

> The reality that few of us like to admit is that we're all terminally ill. If nothing else, old age is a disease that will eventually take all of us.

Ask students to share their initial "gut-level" reaction to this statement. Then make a transition to the next activity: **Though most people don't enjoy talking about the possibility of terminal illness, God wants us to be prepared both to minister to people experiencing it and to be well-prepared for it ourselves.**

Considering Scripture

Group Bible Search
20–25 Minutes

Divide into groups of six to eight. (You might combine already existing groups if you used the first "Community Building" activity.) Appoint a facilitator in each group. Direct the groups to explore how Jesus responded to terminal illness in the family of his friend, Lazarus: **Though many people are familiar with Jesus raising Lazarus from the dead, he also demonstrated some key ways we as Christians should respond when terminal illness enters the lives of people we care about. Read *John 11:1–44* carefully and notice what Jesus did to minister to Lazarus's family.**

After about 15 minutes, ask each group to report how Jesus responded to people experiencing terminal illness. After all the groups have reported, lead a discussion on how Christians can respond in some of the same ways Christ did. Keep the following points in mind as you take the groups' reports and lead the discussion.

JESUS' RESPONSES	OUR RESPONSES
Jesus responded out of love (vv. 3–5).	We need to respond when our friends, family, or church family members are hurting.
Jesus kept an eternal perspective (v. 4).	We are not just concerned people, but God's special people who see death as God does.
Jesus took personal risk to go and be with Lazarus and his family (vv. 8, 16).	Though our risk is not nearly as great as Jesus' was, we need to reach out to others who are grieving even though it might be awkward or uncomfortable to get involved.
Jesus encouraged grieving people with the truth and hope of the resurrection (vv. 25, 40).	We need to be aware of natural "openings" to carefully and compassionately remind people of this hope without coming across as pious or simply handing out platitudes.
Jesus shared their pain (vv. 33, 35, 38).	We need to empathize and validate the pain and heartache people experience.
Jesus prayed for people (v.41).	We can pray with and for people who are hurting. (But we shouldn't force this!)

OPTION
Lecture-Discussion
15 –20 Minutes

You may want to use this option if you have the *Dream Intruders* handbook. Prepare a lecture-discussion from pages 30–32 of *Dream Intruders* on how to help people through the stages of grief that accompany terminal illness. Ask the class, **What are some examples of what it's like to be in these stages?** Or ask, **How did you know when someone you cared about was in these stages?** You might want to use some of the information from the "Considering Scripture" activity above for additional biblical content and application.

Reflecting and Responding

Choral Reading and Reaction
15–20 Minutes

Before class, ask four people to be readers for this activity. Give each one a copy of Resource Sheet 2B. Also have enough copies so each student will have one. Explain to the readers that they will be reading aloud the verses printed on the sheet (except for 1 Thessalonians 4:13–18) and that they will take turns reading. (Reader 1 reads the first verse, reader 2 reads the second verse, then reader 3 reads, then 4, then 1 reads again, and so on.) Encourage them to read their verses with as much feeling, intonation, and emphasis as they can for the verses they are reading.

To move into this part of the lesson, explain, **Now that we have looked at how to help others deal with terminal illness, God also wants us as Christians to be prepared for it.** Then read the following quote from *Dream Intruders* or put it on the chalkboard or overhead and read it to the class.

> **One of the best things all of us can do that will prepare us before an illness hits is to admit our own mortality—we are going to die. . . . Before an illness we need to face the reality of death and then prepare spiritually for what comes after death.**

Then explain, **The best way for us to personally apply the lesson to ourselves is to focus on what the Bible says about two things: the inevitability of death and the certainty of sharing in Christ's victory over death in the resurrection.**

At this point, distribute copies of Resource Sheet 2B and tell the class to either listen or follow along on their sheets until the readers you recruited earlier get to 1 Thessalonians 4:13–18. Then, the whole class will read these verses in unison. (As the reading begins, you might want to play some recorded instrumental music that fits the serious yet triumphant mood of these Scriptures. Beethoven's "Ode to Joy" played on piano or guitar works well.)

After all the verses have been read, either in pairs or groups of three, ask people to respond to the discussion questions that follow the Scripture on the sheet.

Option
Responsive Reading
15 Minutes

Use Resource Sheet 2C to do a responsive reading of the Twenty-third Psalm. Then break into smaller groups of three or four to answer the discussion questions printed at the bottom of the page.

PLAN TWO

Groups

Materials You'll Need For This Session

Resource Sheets 2A and 2B for optional activities

BUILDING COMMUNITY

1. Whose funeral stands out most vividly in your memory? How did the person die? What makes that funeral so memorable to you?

2. OPTION: Use Resource Sheet 2A, "If It Happened to Me," in groups of three or four. See directions in the Classes section to use this activity.

CONSIDERING SCRIPTURE

Tell the group, **The topic of this session is dealing with terminal illness.** Then read ***John 11:1–44*** as a group. Before the Scripture is read, instruct the group to **Notice how Jesus responded to the family of a person who died from a terminal illness.** Then choose from among the questions below to discuss the passage.

1. Why do you think the sisters of Lazarus sent word to Jesus that Lazarus was sick?

2. The Scripture clearly tells us how Jesus felt about Lazarus and his family. How do you think Jesus felt knowing that Lazarus would die in light of the fact that he also knew Lazarus would rise from the dead?

3. How does the parable in verses 9, 10 explain why Jesus was willing to risk death to go to Lazarus's home town?

4. Do Martha's words about believing that Lazarus would rise at the last day (v. 24) sound like she was drawing real comfort from her belief or does it sound more like an acknowledgment of a theological fact?

5. Do you see or hear any difference in Martha's two statements of faith in verses 24 and 27?

6. Is it possible to truly believe in the resurrection and still draw no comfort from it?

Option

Accountability Partners

Ask partners to discuss with each other the following questions this week.

- When was the last time you gave serious thought to the inevitability of your own death?
- What effect does thinking about your own death have on you?
- How has your relationship with God made a difference in how you think or feel about death?

Option

Memory Verse

"I am the resurrection and the life. He who believes in me will live even though he dies" (John 11:25).

7. Since Jesus knew he was about to raise Lazarus from the dead, why was he "deeply moved and troubled," and why did he weep?

8. What does Jesus' weeping at the tomb of Lazarus tell us about how we should comfort people who are grieving even though we know we have the victory over death in Jesus?

9. What is the attitude behind the words of Lazarus's friends in verse 37? Have you or anyone you have known felt this way toward God when illness struck?

10. What is the intended benefit of Jesus' prayer in verses 41, 42?

11. Which of the ways Jesus responded to the family of Lazarus is most important for us as we try to minister to people who have lost someone to a terminal illness?

12. How can reaching out to people with terminal illnesses (or to their families) involve personal risk for us?

13. How should we go about encouraging people with the promise of the resurrection without coming across as sounding pious or failing to appreciate the depth of their pain?

14. Should we always try to pray with people who are grieving? Why or why not?

Reflecting and Responding

Break into smaller groups of no more than four for these more personal questions.

1. If someone you loved was dying of a terminal illness and you knew that person was a Christian, what effect would the promise of the resurrection have on you?

2. When was the last time you gave serious thought to the inevitability of your own death? What effect does thinking about it have on you?

3. If you were to plan your own funeral service, what would you want to have included in it?

4. Option: If there is time, gather the group and pass out copies of Resource Sheet 2B. Sitting or standing in a circle, go around the group and have each person read a verse out loud. Then, when you get to 1 Thessalonians 4:13–18, read it in unison.

If It Happened to Me . . .

Cut out the following scenarios, fold them in half, and place them in a box or small bag. In groups of three or four, have each person draw out a situation, read it to the group, and then answer the questions that go with each situation.

After a routine physical, your doctor tells you that you have contracted an incurable illness. After telling your family, who would you talk to next? Please explain.

Your seven-year-old child has a friend who dies from leukemia. Would you want your child to go to the funeral? How would you try to help your son or daughter understand how such a terrible thing could happen to someone?

Have you ever been concerned that you might have a very serious illness like cancer?

If yes, what kind of thoughts did it make you think? How did you deal with it?

If no, is there any serious illness that you have ever been concerned you might get?

What is the saddest funeral you can remember? What made it so sad?

What is the happiest funeral you can remember? What made it that way?

Copyright © 1995, The Standard Publishing Company. Permission to reproduce for ministry purposes only.

Bad News Good News

The Inevitability of Death and the Certainty of Resurrection

Psalm 89:48
"What man can live and not see death, or save himself from the power of the grave?"

Ecclesiastes 9:5
"For the living know that they will die."

Genesis 3:19
"For dust you are and to dust you will return."

James 4:14
"What is your life? You are a mist that appears for a little while and then vanishes."

Hebrews 9:27
"Man is destined to die once, and after that to face judgment."

1 Corinthians 15:26
"The last enemy to be destroyed is death."

Psalm 90:12
"Teach us to number our days aright, that we may gain a heart of wisdom."

Proverbs 14:32
"When calamity comes, the wicked are brought down, but even in death the righteous have a refuge."

Romans 6:23
"The wages of sin is death, but the gift of God is eternal life in Christ Jesus our Lord."

John 3:16, 17
"For God so loved the world that he gave his one and only Son, that whoever believes in him shall not perish but have eternal life. For God did not send his Son into the world to condemn the world, but to save the world through him."

Philippians 1:21
"For to me, to live is Christ and to die is gain."

1 Corinthians 15: 54, 55
"Death has been swallowed up in victory. Where, O death, is your victory? Where, O death, is your sting?"

John 11:25
Jesus said to her, "I am the resurrection and the life. He who believes in me will live even though he dies."

Revelation 21:4
"He will wipe every tear from their eyes. There will be no more death or mourning."

Revelation 1:18
"I am the Living One; I was dead, and behold I am alive for ever and ever! And I hold the keys of death."

John 10:28
"I give them eternal life, and they shall never perish."

1 Thessalonians 4:13–18
"We do not want you to . . . grieve like the rest of men, who have no hope. We believe that Jesus died and rose again and so we believe that God will bring with Jesus those who have fallen asleep in him. According to the Lord's own word, we tell you that we who are still alive, who are left till the coming of the Lord, will certainly not precede those who have fallen asleep. For the Lord himself will come down from heaven, with a loud command, with the voice of the archangel and with the trumpet call of God, and the dead in Christ will rise first. After that, we who are still alive and are left will be caught up together with them in the clouds to meet the Lord in the air. And so we will be with the Lord forever. Therefore encourage each other with these words."

Questions to Consider

1. How did you feel or what thoughts did you think as you heard the first few verses on the inevitability of death?

2. Which of the verses stood out the most to you? What effect did it have on you to hear these words?

3. If you were to pick any of these Scriptures to be read at your own funeral, which one(s) would you pick?

Copyright © 1995, The Standard Publishing Company. Permission to reproduce for ministry purposes only.

Through the Valley

Leader: *"The Lord is my shepherd, I shall not be in want."*

Response: "He makes me lie down in green pastures, he leads me beside quiet waters."

Leader: *"He restores my soul. He guides me in paths of righteousness for his name's sake."*

Response: "Even though I walk through the valley of the shadow of death, I will fear no evil, for you are with me; your rod and your staff, they comfort me."

Leader: *"You prepare a table before me in the presence of my enemies. You anoint my head with oil; my cup overflows."*

Response: "Surely goodness and love will follow me all the days of my life, and I will dwell in the house of the Lord forever."

—Psalm 23

Questions to Consider

1. If someone you loved was dying of a terminal illness and you knew that person was a Christian, what effect would the promise of the resurrection have on you?

2. When was the last time you gave serious thought to the inevitability of your own death? What effect does thinking about it have on you?

3. If you were to plan your own funeral service, what would you want to have included in it?

Copyright © 1995, The Standard Publishing Company. Permission to reproduce for ministry purposes only.

Dream Intruder #3

The Intruder of
Job Loss

There are many different terms for it. You got a "pink slip." They gave you the "boot." You were asked to "resign." You were "laid off." Your "contract wasn't renewed." There was a "plant closing." But to you it all amounts to the same thing: "You're fired!"

Whether you were asked to submit your resignation or were simply let go, it's the same thing emotionally. No job, no income, no reason to get up each day, no self-worth, and strained family relationships. You've met a dream intruder.

You can look at the dream intruder of losing your job as an enemy, the worst thing that ever happened to you. Or you can face it as an ally and say, "You know, this is an opportunity for me to develop some character." If it was not your fault, you can appreciate your own abilities and start over. If it was your fault, you can begin to make some character adjustments or get some additional training or take some other necessary action to overcome whatever led to your dismissal.

The dream intruder of being fired can be the catalyst to something wonderful in your life. Maybe it's led you to seek the Lord for the first time in a long time. Maybe it's helped you get a fresh perspective on what you want to do the rest of your life. Maybe Christ has given you a new beginning and new motivation.

God's in the business of doing some beautiful work through dream intruders. Being fired is no exception.

—Adapted from *Dream Intruders,* by Gene Appel

Central Theme Though the loss of a job is usually extremely difficult, with God's help we can overcome the pain and grow through the experience.

Lesson Aim Students will appreciate the serious effects of job loss and learn biblical ways of dealing with job loss

Bible Background Ecclesiastes 5:18, 19; James 1:2, 3; 1 Kings 19:1–16; Philippians 3:13, 14

For Further Study Read Dream Intruder #3, "You're Fired!" in *Dream Intruders*.

PLAN ONE

Classes

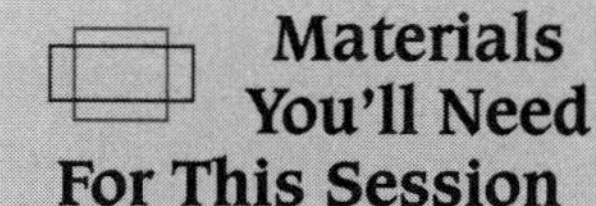

Materials You'll Need For This Session

Copies of Resource Sheets 3A-G, Transparency 3A, and pens or pencils

BUILDING COMMUNITY

Dream Job
5–10 Minutes

To begin class, use the following questions to get people thinking and talking about the important impact our jobs have on our lives: **If you could have any job in the world, which one would you choose and why? How would having your "dream job" make your life better?** Get responses in one large group, in pairs, or in small groups of three or four.

Then make a transition to the next activity: **Our jobs have a tremendous impact on our lives financially, socially, emotionally, and spiritually. This is important to keep in mind today as we focus on dealing with the dream intruder of losing a job.**

OPTION
My Job History
10–15 Minutes

Distribute copies of Resource Sheet 3A, "My Career History," and give class members five minutes to complete the graph on their own. Then divide into groups of three or four so people can share the ups and downs of their careers as a way of focusing the class on how our jobs affect our lives. Then use a transition statement similar to the one above (in "Dream Job") to move on to the next activity.

CONSIDERING SCRIPTURE

Group Research and Report
25–30 Minutes

Explain to the class, **There are three important questions we need to answer to deal effectively with job loss. You will be breaking into three groups. Each group will work on one of the questions on these resource sheets, and then you will briefly report to the class what you have found.**

Divide the class into three groups and distribute copies of Resource Sheets 3B, 3C, and 3D, with one group getting 3B, one getting 3C, and one 3D. Appoint a leader in each group and make sure each group selects someone to give their report to the whole class later. (The reporter might be the leader or not. Leave that up to each group.) Let each group know that they have about 15–20 minutes to do their research.

After each group has had enough time, start with the group that had sheet 3B and get a report. Then do the same with 3C, and then 3D. You might want to take notes on an overhead of the main points each group brings out in their report.

Option
Dealing With Career Crisis
20–25 Minutes

Use Transparency 3A or copy the quote from the transparency master onto the chalkboard. Ask people to either agree or disagree with this statement.

Briefly discuss what a large impact our jobs have on our lives. Explain to the class, **In light of the significance of our jobs, it is no wonder many people find it difficult to cope with the pain of job loss without getting stuck in all the negative thoughts and emotions that come with the territory.** Then explain, **In the biblical account of Elijah the prophet, we have a clear example of how negative thoughts and feelings can overwhelm anyone when things have gone bad in their job and how God can help us overcome them.** (Elijah's greatest success as a prophet was followed up by the greatest threat to his career: the queen of his country wanted him dead.)

Then distribute copies of Resource Sheet 3E and divide into groups of five to ten people. Have the groups read 1 Kings 19:1–16 and discuss the questions that follow on the sheet.

Reflecting and Responding

Dear Me . . .
10–15 Minutes

Distribute copies of Resource Sheet 3F, "Dear Me . . ." to each student. Allow five to ten minutes for each person to complete the note on his or her own. Then ask students to talk to someone on either side of them about the one thing that stands out to them as most important from today's lesson as it applies to their lives.

Option
A Prayer From the Fired
7–10 Minutes

Distribute copies of Resource Sheet 3G, "A Prayer From the Fired," and ask each person to take a few minutes to complete it. Then ask for volunteers to read their prayers to the class.

Plan Two

Groups

Building Community

1. What was the first job you ever had that you received an actual paycheck for? (How old were you? How did you get the job? How did you feel about having your first official job?)

2. How and why did the job end?

3. Option: Use one of the activities from the "Building Community" section of Plan One for Classes.

Considering Scripture

Introduce and explain the topic in this way: **Because jobs are so important in our lives, losing a job can be devastating. God wants to help us respond well to job loss and be ready to help others who experience it. In the Scripture we're going to read, we see what happened to Elijah when his career as a prophet was in jeopardy and how God helped him deal with it.**

Explain briefly the background of the Scripture: **Elijah has just had his greatest career success as a prophet in the famous encounter with the false prophets of Baal at Mt. Carmel. Jezebel is the queen and a follower of Baal.**

Then have someone read ***1 Kings 19:1–16,*** and select from the following questions for group discussion. (If the *Dream Intruders* handbook is available to you, consult pages 41–46 for help in leading this discussion.)

1. Why do you think Elijah was so afraid and fled from Jezebel just after God had so miraculously demonstrated his power through Elijah at Mt. Carmel?

2. How would you paraphrase Elijah's words to God in verse 4?

3. What do verses 5 and 6 tell us that God did first to help Elijah when he was in a crisis?

4. Why did Elijah flee to Mt. Horeb?

Materials You'll Need For This Session

Copies of Resource Sheet 3H

OPTION

Accountability Partners

Distribute copies of Resource Sheet 3F, "Dear Me," for partners to use. Ask them to complete the exercise individually and then get together to share what they came up with. Also, encourage them to share one prayer request about the greatest need they have on their jobs at this time.

OPTION

Memory Verse

"Whatever you do, work at it with all your heart, as working for the Lord, not for men" (Colossians 3:23).

5. How much time elapsed between the onset of Elijah's depression and when God spoke to him at Mt. Horeb?

6. How are Elijah's feelings and thoughts in verse 10 similar to the way people think and feel after they get fired?

7. Why does Elijah repeat himself to the Lord in verse 14? Why say this again?

8. How do you think Elijah felt when God told him to go out and stand on the mountain because he was about to pass by?

9. After the powerful wind, the earthquake, and the fire did not have the Lord in them, do you think it surprised Elijah that God was found in a gentle whisper?

10. What impact do you think the new mission God gave Elijah in verses 15, 16 had on all the negative things Elijah was thinking and feeling?

REFLECTING AND RESPONDING

Divide into groups of no more than four people. Distribute one copy of Resource Sheet 3H to each group. Direct half of the groups to discuss Set A and half to discuss Set B. Let each group know when they need to finish by. When all the groups are finished, ask volunteers from each group to summarize their discussions.

Close in prayer.

My Job History

Chart the ups and downs of your work life since you finished school. Make a line graph that shows your highs and lows over the years that are associated with your career.

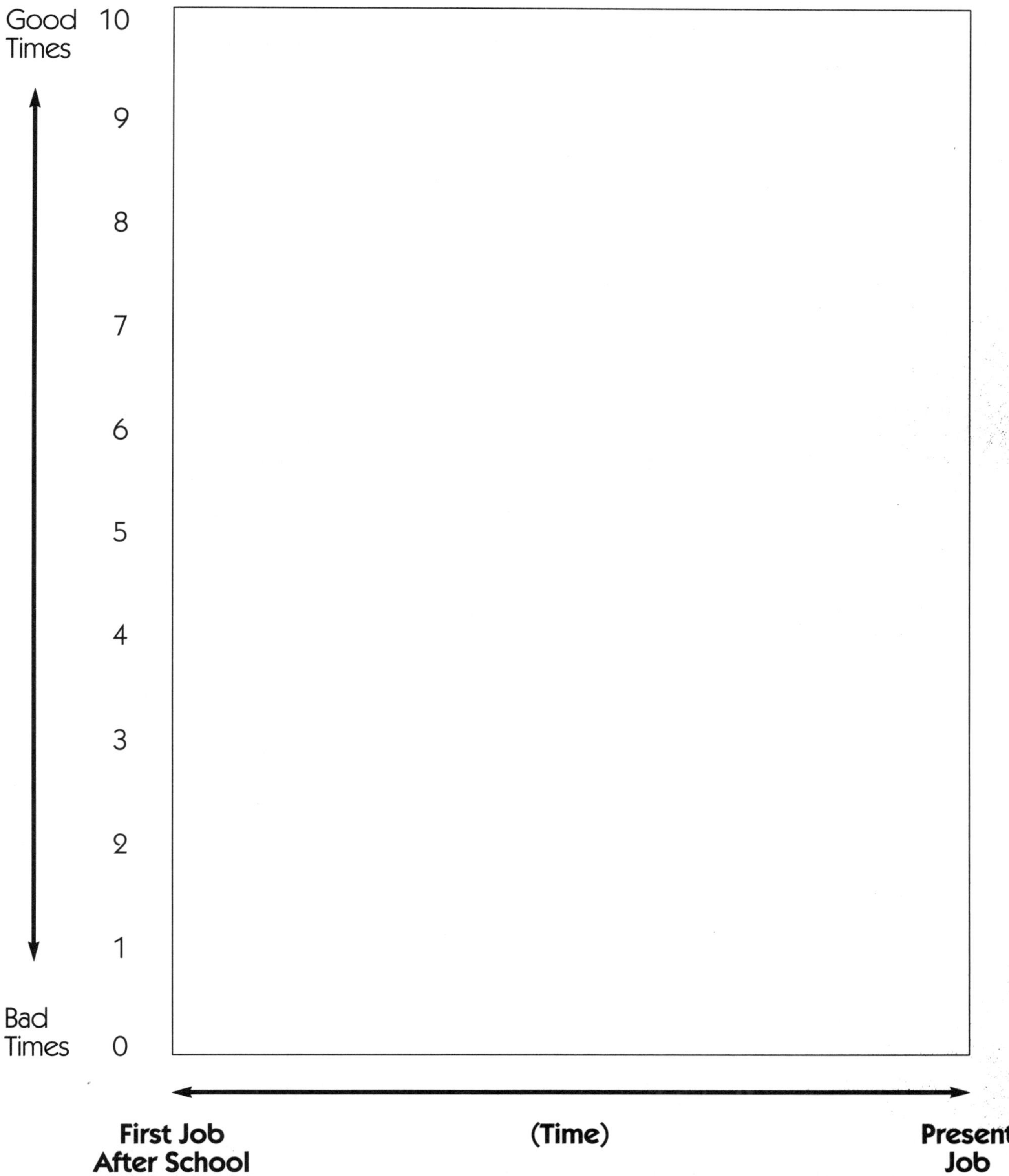

Copyright © 1995, The Standard Publishing Company. Permission to reproduce for ministry purposes only.

"Why Did I Lose My Job?"

Read the following quotes from the book *Dream Intruders* on job loss and discuss the questions that follow.

Why was I fired? This question is critical, because an honest answer will help you gain an important perspective on your situation. The reason you lost your job may have nothing to do with you, or it may have everything to do with you. So take some time, evaluate honestly, and ask, "Why was I fired?"

1. List as many reasons as you can that people lose their jobs, including things that are their fault and things that are not.

2. What would you say to someone who said after losing a job, "It doesn't matter whose fault it was. The past is the past. I've got to move on and find a new job"?

Were you at fault when you lost your job? When you are able to answer that question honestly, you are making your first major step toward getting through this dream intruder. If it was not your fault, you can appreciate your own abilities and start over. If it was your fault, you can begin to make some character adjustments or get some additional training or take some other necessary action to overcome whatever led to your dismissal.

3. Can the question of "Was I at fault?" only be answered on your own, or are there additional ways to come to an honest answer?

4. There are two main mistakes one can make in answering the question, "Was I at fault?" One is to refuse to accept responsibility and put the blame on someone else when it was your fault. The other is to wrongly put the blame on yourself when it was predominantly not your fault.
   Which of these mistakes do you think is easier to fall into for most Christians?

5. How can God help us to answer the question, "Was I at fault?" openly and honestly?

Copyright © 1995, The Standard Publishing Company. Permission to reproduce for ministry purposes only.

"How Can I Beat This Depression?"

Depression is a very common reaction to the loss of a job. Read 1 Kings 19:1–16 and look for two sets of things: (1) symptoms of Elijah's depression and (2) God's ways of helping Elijah out of his depression.

Elijah's Depression

Verse 3:

Verse 4:

Verse 5:

Verse 10:

Verse 14:

God's Help For Elijah

Verse 4:

Verses 5, 6:

Verse 9:

Verse 11:

Verse 12:

Verses 15, 16:

Copyright © 1995, The Standard Publishing Company. Permission to reproduce for ministry purposes only.

"How Can I Move Forward?"

Read the following Scriptures and the quote from the book *Dream Intruders* and answer the questions below to explore how God can help us move forward after a devastating loss.

Paul's Past

Both previous job successes and failures can keep us from moving forward after a job is lost. The apostle Paul had both good and bad experiences in his career before becoming an apostle. The bad things are summed up in ***Acts 26:9–11,*** and his successes are listed in ***Philippians 3:4–6.*** Read those two passages, and discuss the questions below.

1. How could Paul's successes in his previous career have kept him from moving forward?

2. How could Paul's failures in his previous career have kept him from moving forward?

God's Prescription for Paul

"But one thing I do: Forgetting what is behind and straining toward what is ahead, I press on toward the goal to win the prize for which God has called me heavenward in Christ Jesus."

—Philippians 3:13, 14

3. Do you think Paul actually forgot what had happened in his old life before God gave him his new job? If he did think about the past (good and bad), how do you think his new goal helped him think about it differently?

"Maybe the reason you lost your job was not your fault, but then again, maybe it was. Whatever the reason, God can still give you a new purpose and a new direction. Let God give you a new direction for your life. He's not through with you. As a Christian, you will find he gives you a new purpose and a new meaning in living. You need something greater to live for than just yourself. You need something greater to draw you out of yourself. And that is a vital relationship with Christ."

—Gene Appel, *Dream Intruders*

4. What examples can you think of from your own life or the lives of people you've known that demonstrate how a vital relationship with Christ can give us a new direction and purpose after something serious like job loss?

Copyright © 1995, The Standard Publishing Company. Permission to reproduce for ministry purposes only.

Questions
TO CONSIDER

Depression is a very common reaction to the loss of a job. Read 1 Kings 19:1–16, and then answer the questions below.

1. Which of Elijah's reactions to his situation do you think are easiest for you to fall into?

2. Which of the ways that God helped Elijah when he was in crisis do you think would be most difficult for you to take advantage of?

3. If you lost your job and God said something particular to help you make it through, what do you think he might say?

4. What difference would ministering to others have on you if you lost your job?

Copyright © 1995, The Standard Publishing Company. Permission to reproduce for ministry purposes only.

Dear Me . . .

There are four main things God wants us to do when job loss comes our way:

1. Take care of ourselves physically (1 Kings 19:6–8).
2. Be open and honest with God in prayer about what we think and feel (1 Kings 19:10, 14).
3. Allow God to speak to us (1 Kings 19:9–16).
4. Reach out in ministry to others (1 Kings 19:15, 16).

Finish writing yourself the encouraging note below. Base it on the things discussed in today's lesson, which might help you if you ever lose your job.

Dear Me:

Since you are reading this note now, it means you probably just lost your job. I wanted to write you this note to encourage you through this very difficult time.

Copyright © 1995, The Standard Publishing Company. Permission to reproduce for ministry purposes only.

A Prayer from the Fired

Write a prayer to God as if you just lost your job. Base it on the things presented in today's lesson.

Dear God:

I just lost my job . . .

In Jesus' Name,
Amen.

Copyright © 1995, The Standard Publishing Company. Permission to reproduce for ministry purposes only.

Honest with God

Set A

1. Have you ever lost a job or had things go so bad with your job that you felt as Elijah did when he sat under the tree and told God, "I've had enough; take my life"?

2. Is it easy or hard for you to be honest and open (as Elijah was) with God about how you really feel? Why or why not?

3. Of the ways that God helped Elijah in his time of need, which do you think you would need most from God if you lost your job or were dealing with something as serious as job loss?

4. What can we do to make sure we hear what God wants us to hear when we are in distress?

Set B

Here are the four main things God did to help Elijah out of his crisis:

- took care of him physically with food, water, and rest (vv. 6–8)
- allowed him to vent his thoughts and feelings honestly about his situation (vv. 10, 14)
- spoke to him (vv. 9–16)
- sent him to minister to others (vv. 15, 16)

1. Which of the four things do you think would be most important to you if you lost your job? (If you already have had this experience, did any of these help you?)

2. If you lost your job and God said something particular to help you make it through, what do think he would say to you?

3. Do you find it easy or hard to speak your mind and heart openly to God as Elijah did? What makes it easy or hard for you to do this?

4. What difference would ministering to others have on you if you lost your job?

Copyright © 1995, The Standard Publishing Company. Permission to reproduce for ministry purposes only.

THE TRAUMA *of Job Loss*

"Then I realized that it is good and proper for a man to eat and drink, and to find satisfaction in toilsome labor under the sun during the few days of life God has given him—for this is his lot. Moreover, when God gives any man wealth and possessions, and enables him to enjoy them, to accept his lot and be happy in his work—this is a gift of God."

—Ecclesiastes 5:18, 19

"Believe the surveys claiming that, next to the death of a loved one, losing a job is the most traumatic experience most of us endure."

—Lou Nell Bath (after being fired)
"What a Wonderful Web He Weaves"
The Lookout, November 12, 1989

Copyright © 1995, The Standard Publishing Company. Permission to reproduce for ministry purposes only.

Dream Intruder #4

The Intruder of
Prodigal Children

It seems most families have at least one child who ends up breaking the parents' heart one day. You always thought, "That won't be my child. Other people have prodigal children, but not me." Then it happens to you. Maybe it begins with a series of incidents. Or maybe it's one big jolt. Your child runs away. Your daughter is arrested. Your son is selling drugs. Your child leaves her husband and runs off to who knows where with another man. Your son informs you he is gay and wants nothing to do with you, your life, or your values.

"Why did this happen to my child?" We could list peer pressure, the state of our world, lack of discipline, abuse, and many others. But it is very important that you understand that everything we've just listed is an influence and not a cause. Your actions influence your child's behavior. But that's all it is: influence. You don't cause your child's behavior.

Are you a hurting parent? Then remember our heavenly Father has prodigal children, too. You probably can begin to understand better than anyone else just a little bit of the heartbreak God must feel over the billions of prodigal children in the world.

Remember: behavior is not going to change until a person's heart changes. There's no use arguing about the person's behavior, because people out of step with God are not going to act and walk as if they actually are in step with him. Your goal is that your child who is spiritually lost be spiritually found. —Adapted from *Dream Intruders,* by Gene Appel

Central Theme Though parents may not be responsible for their adult children's actions, they are called by God to love and witness to their prodigal children.

Lesson Aims Students will learn from Scripture that parents do not *cause* children's' bad choices and they will identify where they need to grow to respond in obedience to Scripture when they are in this situation.

Bible Background 1 Samuel 3:19–21; 7:3–14; 8:1–5; Luke 15:11–24

For Further Study Read Dream Intruder #4, "Prodigal Children," in *Dream Intruders*.

PLAN ONE

Classes

BUILDING COMMUNITY

Brainstorming
5–10 Minutes

Read or display the following quote from the book *Dream Intruders*:

> **It seems that most families have at least one child who ends up breaking the parents' heart one day. You always thought, "That won't be my child. Other people have prodigal children, but not me." Then it happens to you. Maybe it begins with a series of incidents. Or maybe it's one big jolt. Your child runs away. Your daughter is arrested. Your son is selling drugs. Your child leaves her husband and runs off to who knows where with another man. Your son informs you he is gay and wants nothing to do with you, your life, or your values. "Why did this happen to my child?"**

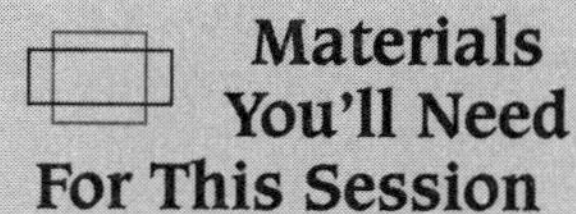

Materials You'll Need For This Session

Copies of Resource Sheets 4A–C, Transparency 4A, and pens or pencils

Ask the class to brainstorm as many answers as they can to the "Why?" question of prodigal children. Then make a transition to the next activity: **As we begin looking at the problem of prodigal children, it's important to understand that though there are many influences on our kids' behavior, the Bible shows us that the course our kids choose to take is ultimately their own responsibility. In the Bible, the children of even the most committed, exemplary parents sometimes took paths in life that were totally the opposite of what they were taught.** (For background on this point, you may want to read pages 58–60 of *Dream Intruders.)*

OPTION
Neighbor Nudge
5 Minutes

Ask people to talk to the person sitting next to them about the following question: **What is the most trouble you ever got into before you were 18?**

Then make a transition to the next activity: **We all got into trouble of one kind or another. Maybe even some of us would qualify at one time in our lives as prodigal children. Our class today is on the dream intruder of prodigal children, and the Bible shows us that any parents, no matter how good of parents they are, can have prodigal children.**

Considering Scripture

Mini-Lecture
5–10 Minutes

Distribute copies of Resource Sheet 4A, "Samuel and Sons." Ask students to follow along as you ask for volunteers to look up and read the Scriptures listed on the sheet, which show the kind of person Samuel was and the way his sons decided to live their lives. Then discuss as a group the questions at the bottom of the page. Move on to the next activity by pointing out that **Whether or not we feel we did a good job of raising our kids, we still have to be ready to relate to them as God wants us to.**

Group Bible Search and Report
15 Minutes

Distribute copies of Resource Sheet 4B, "Prescription for Parents of Prodigals," and divide the class into groups of six to eight to complete the sheet. Appoint a facilitator in each group and let each group know how much time this activity will take.

After the groups have finished, bring the class back together. Beginning with the first Scripture on the sheet, go around to each group to hear what do's or don'ts they found in each one. You might want to write these down on the chalkboard as you go. Or, as another option, use Transparency 4A to lead the discussion, uncovering one principle at a time as you go. (If the *Dream Intruders* handbook is available to you, refer to pages 60–63 for background.)

Option
Group Discussion
25 Minutes

Lead a group discussion of the parable of the prodigal son (Luke 15:11–24), choosing from among the questions listed in the Groups section of this lesson. Bring out the following points in the discussion: **The father was waiting for the son to come home; the father took the initiative to reach out to his son; the father greeted the son warmly and lovingly even before he knew his son had decided to change; the father focused on the son being found; the father did not condemn his son for his behavior; the father was open in front of others about his love for his son.**

Reflecting and Responding

Drama Groups
15 Minutes

If you did the first option under "Considering Scripture," get the class back into groups and distribute to each group one of the scenarios from Resource Sheet 4C. Ask each group to do two brief skits: one on how *not* to respond to the scenario and one on how *to* respond to the scenario. Encourage them to "ham up" the how-not-to-do-it skits for fun.

Small Group Discussion
15 Minutes

Make copies of Resource Sheet 4C, and hand out one scenario to each student. Divide into groups of three or four and ask each person to read his or her scenario. Write the following questions on the chalkboard or overhead for each person to answer in the groups. (The students will need to refer to the list of do's and don'ts they came up with earlier on the "Prescriptions for Parents" resource sheet. If you wrote the list on the chalkboard, do not erase it before doing this activity. Or, as another option, you can use Transparency 4A for this activity.)

- Which of the do's and don'ts would be easiest for you to do if you were in the situation you were given? Why?
- Which of the do's and don'ts would be most difficult for you? Why?
- In what ways do you need to grow so that if this happened to you, you could do what God wants you to do in your relationship with your child?

Plan Two

Groups

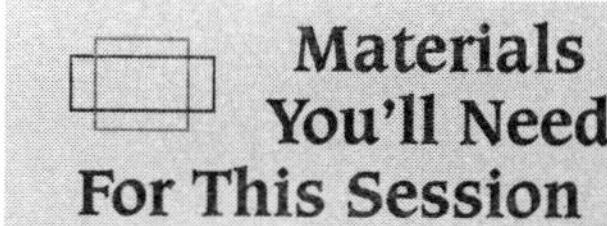

Materials You'll Need For This Session

Resource Sheets 4C and 4D and Transparency 4A

Premeeting

Before the meeting, call everyone in the group. Ask each person to tell you his or her most embarrassing moment as a child (before age 18). It should be something no one else in the group (besides a spouse) would know about. It could be something they did or something that happened to them. Ask them not to share it with anyone before the next meeting. Write down brief descriptions of their stories so you can read them to the group. Omit any facts that might give away who the story belongs to.

Building Community

1. Read the stories one at a time to the group. Ask people to guess who the story belongs to, and don't reveal it until everyone has had a chance to guess. Then tell whose story it is and allow that person to add a few details of how and why it happened. Then go on to the next story and do the same until all the stories have been read.

2. Option: **Did you ever run away or threaten to run away from home when you were a child? What were the circumstances?**

Considering Scripture

Today we're looking at the subject of prodigal children and how God wants us to respond to our kids when they choose a way of life that leads them away from both us and the life God wants them to be living. Let's look together at the most famous biblical example of a wayward child to learn what God wants us to do and not to do in this difficult situation. Then have someone read ***Luke 15:11–24*** out loud and choose from among the following questions to guide the discussion.

1. If one of your kids asked for what the younger son asked for, how would you respond?

2. Why do you think the father complied with his son's request?

3. When the prodigal son left with the money, do you think the father should have felt responsible, since he was the one who gave him the money in the first place?

4. The parable doesn't say whether or not the father tried to stop his son from leaving. Based on what you know of the father from this passage, do you think he tried to stop him, or just let him go? (If you think he tried to stop him, how do you think he would have gone about it?)

5. What do you think the father was doing so that he was able to see his son while he was "still a long way off"? What does this tell us about the father?

6. What does it tell us about the father that he was filled with compassion at the sight of his son? What else could he have felt at that moment?

7. What do you suppose the son thought when he saw his father running toward him?

8. Why didn't the father simply wait for his son to come to him instead of running out to greet him?

9. What is the father's response to the son's repentance speech?

10. What things did the father *not* do that most people would have done when the son returned home?

11. Option: Read the parable of the prodigal son aloud. Then hand out copies of Resource Sheet 4B, "Prescription for Parents of Prodigals." Divide into two or three smaller groups. Then do this activity according to the instructions under "Considering Scripture" in the Classes section of this lesson.

Reflecting and Responding

1. Make copies of Resource Sheet 4C and Transparency 4A. Hand out one scenario from the resource sheet to each person. Divide into groups of three or four people and ask each person to read his or her scenario. Briefly go over the "Guidelines for Parents of Prodigals," listed on Transparency 4A. (These come from pages 60–63 of the *Dream Intruders* handbook.) Then ask each person to read the scenario to the group and answer the following questions.

- Which of the guidelines would be easiest for you to follow if you were in the situation you were given? Why?
- Which of the guidelines would be most difficult for you? Why?
- In what ways do you need to grow so that if this did happen to you, you could do what God wants you to do in your relationship with your child?

2. Option: Divide into two or three smaller groups and pass out a copy of Resource Sheet 4D, "The Parable of the Waiting Father," to each person. Have the smaller group discuss these questions.

Option

Accountability Partners

Ask accountability partners to discuss the following two questions:

- Has there been a prodigal child in your family?
- What do you think is the most important thing for a Christian parent of a prodigal child to understand?

Option

Memory Verse

"Above all, love each other deeply, because love covers over a multitude of sins" (1 Peter 4:8).

Samuel and Sons

Sometimes parents can be terrific role models and godly people, and their children still become prodigals. The following Scriptures tell us about the kind of person Samuel was and how his children chose to live their lives.

SAMUEL

1 Samuel 3:19–21

1 Samuel 7:3–6

1 Samuel 7:7–11

1 Samuel 7:12–14

Psalm 99:6, 7

SAMUEL'S SONS

1 Samuel 8:1–5

Questions to Consider . . .

1. Which of Samuel's attributes do you think had the most potential to make him a good father?

2. How is it possible that a man who was so close to God could have sons who turned out as Samuel's did?

3. What examples do you know of where good parents still experienced the pain of a prodigal child?

4. What difference can it make for the parents of prodigal children to understand that parents are not accountable for their children's choices?

Copyright © 1995, The Standard Publishing Company. Permission to reproduce for ministry purposes only.

PRESCRIPTION FOR Parents of Prodigals

Look up the following verses to find guidelines for parents of prodigal children.

	DO'S	DON'TS
James 1:19		
1 John 3:18		
Ephesians 4:2		
1 Corinthians 16:14		
Romans 12:3		
Romans 15:7		
1 Peter 4:8		
Matthew 5:16		
Philippians 4:8		
Colossians 4:6		

Copyright © 1995, The Standard Publishing Company. Permission to reproduce for ministry purposes only.

Your 26-year-old daughter calls to tell you she is leaving your son-in-law, to whom she has been married for about three years. He has been like part of the family. She admits that he has done almost everything a good husband should, but she says she just doesn't want to be married anymore. You find out "through the grapevine" that she is now living with a man she has been having an affair with for the last six months.

Your 17-year-old son, who will be eighteen in less than six months, announces that he doesn't believe in God anymore and that he never really did in the first place. He refuses to have anything to do with your church, and he says you are being naive and simpleminded to believe "all that stuff." He goes on to say that as soon as he is old enough, he is moving out so he can live his own life.

You get a call late one Saturday night from the local police department. The officer informs you your 18-year-old daughter has been arrested for drunk driving. When you get to the station, your daughter says she has been drinking heavily for the last couple of years and that you just didn't care enough to notice. She says she's always been unhappy and the drinking is all your fault because you haven't done a better job as a parent. Weeks later she continues to tell you she sees things this way.

Your 25-year-old son has been overseas with the military for the last two and a half years. One day you receive a letter from him. He says he has finally decided to "come out of the closet" about his homosexuality. He has a leave coming up in the summer and wants to come home for a two-week visit.

Copyright © 1995, The Standard Publishing Company. Permission to reproduce for ministry purposes only.

The Parable of the Waiting Father

Some have said the parable of the prodigal son is really more about the father than the son. Take a few minutes to answer the following questions to reflect and respond to the Scripture.

1. Which of the following would be most difficult for you to deal with as the parent of a prodigal?

- ❑ the embarrassment if others knew
- ❑ my own sense of failure as a parent
- ❑ anger at my child for messing up
- ❑ trusting enough to open up again
- ❑ other: ________________________________

2. What did the father do that would have been hardest for you to do if you had been in his place?

3. What difference would it make in how you respond to a prodigal child if your perspective was that you spiritually have been a prodigal son or daughter of God? Have you recently been aware of God's patience with you as his child?

4. What stands out to you most from this lesson?

Copyright © 1995, The Standard Publishing Company. Permission to reproduce for ministry purposes only.

Guidelines for Parents of Prodigals

Focus on the Person, Not the Behavior
Ephesians 4:2; Romans 15:7; 1 Peter 4:8

Be Quick to Listen and Slow to Speak or Get Angry
James 1:19

Don't Argue About Behavior
1 John 3:18

Share Your Testimony About God's Grace in Jesus Christ
Matthew 5:16; Colossians 4:6

Copyright © 1995, The Standard Publishing Company. Permission to reproduce for ministry purposes only.

Dream Intruder #5

The Intruder of
Bankruptcy

The terms "chapter 7" and "chapter 13" may sound like sections in a book to some people. To many others, the only book they bring to mind might be a Stephen King novel, for they've experienced the real-life horror of personal bankruptcy. Many who have experienced this dream intruder testify it was like a snowball that turned into an avalanche as they were sliding down a mountain. There was an accident, a health problem, an unforeseen mishap that brought tremendous financial pressures, eventually leading to bankruptcy. Now they have lost everything: their business, their home, their family, and their self-esteem.

Whether you've experienced bankruptcy or not, there are lessons all of us can learn along the way. Most of us are guilty of two common mistakes. The first is a consumptive lifestyle. A consumptive lifestyle is spending more than you can afford. The second common mistake is the lack of a budget. If you don't have a budget, you will tend to buy impulsively.

Jesus said in Luke 14:28, "Suppose one of you wants to build a tower. Will he not first sit down and estimate the cost to see if he has enough money to complete it?" That's pretty basic advice, isn't it? Jesus is simply cautioning us against getting in over our heads.

Analyze your situation. How much is enough? How big does your house need to be? How expensive a car will it take to satisfy you? Good money management begins with a money manager who counts the cost.

—Adapted from *Dream Intruders* by Gene Appel

Central Theme To avoid the danger of bankruptcy, we need to listen to God's Word on finances and spending.

Lesson Aims Students will become aware of the dangers of excessive indebtedness, explore God's commands on spending and borrowing, and identify one of God's commands to apply to their lives.

Bible Background Proverbs 21:5; 21:20; 22:7; Luke 12:15; 14:28; Romans 13:8

For Further Study Read Dream Intruder #5, "Bankruptcy," in *Dream Intruders*.

Plan One

Classes

Building Community

True-False Quiz
10 Minutes

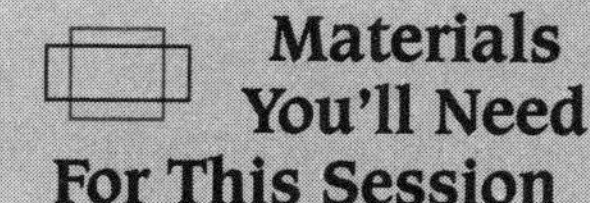

Materials You'll Need For This Session

Copies of Resource Sheets 5A and 5B, a dollar bill, several broad-tip markers, and several poster-board rectangles

Distribute a copy of Resource Sheet 5A, "Money American-Style," to each person in the class. Tell the class, **Since today's lesson is about personal finances, we will all get a chance to test our awareness of some of the facts about Americans and money by taking a simple quiz.** Encourage students to work in pairs, and let them know there will be a prize for the pair who gets the most answers correct.

After there has been enough time to complete the quiz, bring the group back together and begin going over the statements. Read a statement out loud, and then ask students to raise their hands to vote true or false.

Here are the correct answers:

1. False. *Eighty* percent of people in the U.S. have more debts than assets.
2. False. *Eighty-five* percent of Americans have less than $250 when they reach age 65.
3. True.
4. False. According to the Federal Reserve, Americans are carrying *more than $600 billion* in consumer debt.
5. True.
6. True.
7. True.
8. True.
9. False. One out of every *two hundred* Americans files for bankruptcy.
10. False. Many people never tell family and friends that they have declared bankruptcy.

After you have completed going through the answers, find out which pair had the most correct responses. If there is only one winning team, give the pair a dollar bill to split. If several tie for first, divide a dollar in change among them.

Tell the class, **Today's topic is the problem mentioned in the last three items on the quiz: bankruptcy.** Read the following quote from *Dream Intruders* at this point, or say something similar as a transition to the next activity.

> **The terms "chapter 7" and "chapter 13" may sound like sections in a book to some people. To many others, the only book they bring to mind might be a Stephen King**

novel, for they've experienced the real-life horror of personal bankruptcy. . . . Many who have experienced this dream intruder testify it was like a snowball that turned into an avalanche as they were sliding down a mountain. There was an accident, a health problem, an unforeseen mishap that brought tremendous financial pressures, eventually leading to bankruptcy. Now they have lost everything: their business, their home, their family, and their self-esteem. . . .

Whether you've experienced personal bankruptcy or not, there are some important lessons all of us can learn along the way.

Mini-Discussion
5–10 Minutes

One thing we all have in common—whether we have been through bankruptcy or not—is that we live in an era where materialism, poor financial management, and poor stewardship of the resources God gives to people has reached epidemic proportions.

Take a few minutes at this point to let people respond to this question: **Many people believe that declaring bankruptcy will solve their financial difficulties. But the reality is that it can create more problems. What are the negative effects of bankruptcy on people and our society?**

Considering Scripture

Paraphrasing and Matching
30–35 Minutes

As Christians, we need to listen to what people who have experienced bankruptcy often say: "I didn't know how deep into debt I was really getting. I didn't see it coming." One reason people fall into bankruptcy is that they do what the world says to do: "Take on the maximum debt load you can afford—and usually a little more." Then some unexpected financial crisis like a job loss or a serious illness hits and they can't meet all their financial commitments. We need to be keenly aware of the messages the world sends us about how to manage our money versus what God's Word says.

Distribute copies of Resource Sheet 5B, "Who to Listen To?" Divide into groups of six to eight people. Appoint a leader in each group. Direct them to read the directions on the sheets, and then give the groups 20–25 minutes to do the paraphrasing and matching.

After the groups have finished working on the sheets, gather everyone back together. Ask the first group to read the first Scripture, share their paraphrase, and tell what they matched it to as the opposite of what the world says. Then go to group two and do the same thing with the second Scripture, and so on until all the Scriptures have been read and paraphrased. (It's acceptable for the groups to match up different Scriptures with different worldly messages. There is not necessarily one correct match for each one.)

Reflecting and Responding

Discussion in Pairs or Groups
15 Minutes

Give the students a few minutes on their own to rate each of the sayings on Resource Sheet 5B on a scale from 1 to 10 based on how tempted they are to listen to what the world says about finances and spending. Also, ask them to pick which message from God they need most to apply to their lives in their area of finances and spending.

Have students get back into their original pairings from the "Building Community" activity. (Another option is to form small groups of three or four people.) Ask the groups to share two things: which message from the world they rated as the most tempting for them to listen to and which message from God applies most directly to their lives.

Option
Bumper Stickers
15 Minutes

Divide into groups of four to six and ask them to think of themselves as slogan writers for an advertising firm that is trying to interest people in God's wisdom on spending and borrowing. Distribute to each group several broad-tip markers and several poster-board rectangles. (Before class you will need to cut poster board into large bumper-sticker shapes. Each group needs more than one rectangle in case of mistakes.) Instruct them to pick from the Scripture verses studied today the one they think best represents what most Christians need to hear from God. They should then turn that verse into a slogan to put on their bumper sticker. After the groups have finished, ask them to display their bumper stickers and tell which Scriptures or scriptural principles they are trying to get across to people, and why they picked the ones they did.

PLAN TWO

Groups

BUILDING COMMUNITY

1. What is the most important thing you have ever let someone borrow from you? Was it easy or hard to entrust this thing to the person you lent it to?

2. OPTION: Use the "Money American-Style" quiz from Resource Sheet 5A. Follow the instructions from the Classes plan under "Building Community."

CONSIDERING SCRIPTURE

• If you use the first "Building Community" activity above, you might want to use some of the statistics from the optional activity as a segue from the opening question. Then say, **Most of us at one time or another have lent something to someone, and we were concerned we might not get it back. Bankruptcy puts us on the other side: We end up not returning something of value that we promised to give back—plus interest! Though most of us have never or will never experience bankruptcy, it is easy in our society today to fall into one of the main contributors to bankruptcy: overindebtedness. Let's see what the Bible has to say about the subject.**

• OPTION: If you use the "Money American-Style" quiz, also use the transition material suggested with it in the Classes section.

• Distribute a copy of Resource Sheet 5C, "God Speaks on Buying and Borrowing," to each group member. Go around the group, letting people take turns reading the passages of Scripture out loud. Then build a discussion, selecting from the following questions.

1. How does haste lead to poverty?

2. How do people's budgets today reflect the truth of Proverbs 21:20?

3. What does it mean that the borrower is servant to the lender? What examples of this truth do you see in everyday life today?

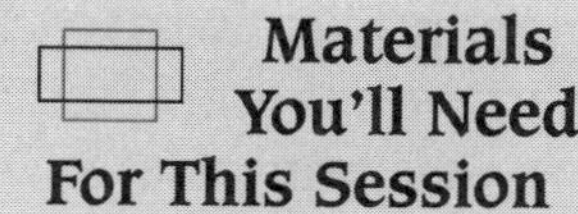

Materials You'll Need For This Session

Copies of Resource Sheets 5C and 5D and, if you use the optional activities, copies of 5A and 5B, several broad-tip markers, and several poster-board rectangles

Option

Accountability Partners

Ask accountability partners to discuss questions two and three from Resource Sheet 5D. Suggest that they also discuss and pray about what each most needs prayer for in their financial lives.

Option

Memory Verse

"Watch out! Be on your guard against all kinds of greed; a man's life does not consist in the abundance of his possessions" (Luke 12:15).

As another option for the memory verse this week, have each participant choose the Bible verse from Resource Sheet 5C that is the biggest challenge for him or her.

4. How would you paraphrase Romans 13:8?

5. In what situations might we find ourselves letting a debt remain outstanding?

6. What would be a modern-day parallel of Jesus' question in Luke 14:28?

7. What different kinds of greed are there?

8. What does it mean to "be on guard against greed"?

9. Why do you think God considers avoiding debt to be in our best interest?

10. Which of these verses do you think is most different from what the world believes?

11. Option: Use Resource Sheet 5B. Follow the instructions under "Considering Scripture" in the Classes section.

Reflecting and Responding

Break into smaller groups of three or four and discuss these questions found on Resource Sheet 5D.

1. Where does the most pressure to buy things that are more than you can afford come from?

- **a. from co-workers' lifestyles**
- **b. from growing up in a poor family**
- **c. from growing up in a rich family**
- **d. from my Christian friends**
- **e. from my family**
- **f. from commercials and advertisements**
- **g. from boredom**
- **h. from wanting to escape feeling bad**
- **i. other:____________________**

2. If a person's life does not consist in the abundance of possessions, what *does* it consist of?

3. Which of the verses we studied speaks most clearly to your financial situation right now?

What steps would you need to take to respond to this verse?

4. Option: Use the "Bumper Sticker" activity from "Reflecting and Responding" in the Classes section.

MONEY "American-Style"

Test your awareness of the personal financial situation in America by circling True or False after each statement.

1. Sixty-five percent of Americans have more debts than assets.[1] **True** **False**

2. Seventy-five percent of Americans have less than $250 in savings when they reach age 65.[1] **True** **False**

3. There is 31 times as much consumer debt now as there was in 1945.[2] **True** **False**

4. Americans carry $50 billion in consumer debt, which doesn't include home mortgages.[1] **True** **False**

5. The average American spends 10 times as much money paying interest on debt each year than on giving to charitable organizations.[2] **True** **False**

6. Seventy-five percent of Americans age 65 and over depend on charity and family to pay their bills. [1] **True** **False**

7. The average American has seven credit cards with a total of $3,000 due on them.[1] **True** **False**

8. From 1984 to 1991, the number of personal bankruptcy filings rose every year.[4] **True** **False**

9. One out of every 400 Americans files for bankruptcy.[5] **True** **False**

10. Because public opinion is more accepting, people are now more likely to be open and talk about the fact that they have gone through bankruptcy.[6] **True** **False**

1. Gene Appel, *Dream Intruders,* pp. 65–69.
2. Randy Alcorn, *Money, Possessions, and Eternity.*
3. *Fortune,* December 30, 1991.
4. *Business Week,* December 10, 1990.
5. *Facts on File,* March 12, 1992.
6. *Minneapolis–St. Paul Magazine,* October 1993

Copyright © 1995, The Standard Publishing Company. Permission to reproduce for ministry purposes only.

Who to Listen To?

"For the wisdom of this world is foolishness in God's sight."
—1 Corinthians 3:19

On the left are several messages from the world we all hear regularly about spending, saving, debt, and possessions. On the right are several passages that sum up what God says to us on the same subjects. Look up the Scriptures one at a time, then work together as a group to paraphrase what the verses are saying about how to manage money and possessions from God's perspective. Then draw a line from the Scripture on the right to its counterpart, what the world says, on the left.

The World Says . . .	**But God Says . . .**
"Your standard of living is the key to your happiness."	Proverbs 21:5
"Buy now; no need to wait."	Luke 14:28
"Charge it! You'll figure out some way to pay for it later."	Proverbs 21:20
"You only go around once, so enjoy it while you can."	Proverbs 22:7b
"If you can't pay for it, don't worry; they can wait to get their money."	Luke 12:15
"As long as you can make the payments, it doesn't matter how much you owe."	Romans 13:8

Copyright © 1995, The Standard Publishing Company. Permission to reproduce for ministry purposes only.

ON BUYING AND BORROWING

"The plans of the diligent lead to profit
as surely as haste leads to poverty."
—Proverbs 21:5

"In the house of the wise are stores of choice food and oil,
but a foolish man devours all he has."
—Proverbs 21:20

"The rich rule over the poor, and the borrower
is servant to the lender."
—Proverbs 22:7

"Let no debt remain outstanding."
—Romans 13:8

"Suppose one of you wants to build a tower. Will he
not first sit down and estimate the cost to see if he has
enough money to complete it?"
—Luke 14:28

"Watch out! Be on your guard against all kinds of greed;
a man's life does not consist in the abundance
of his possessions."
—Luke 12:15

Copyright © 1995, The Standard Publishing Company. Permission to reproduce for ministry purposes only.

Taking Stock of Money Matters

Apply the Scriptures to your own life by answering the following questions.

1. Where does the most pressure to buy things that are more than you can afford come from?
   a. from co-workers' lifestyles
   b. from growing up in a poor family
   c. from growing up in a rich family
   d. from my Christian friends
   e. from my family
   f. from commercials and advertisements
   g. from boredom
   h. from wanting to escape feeling bad
   i. other:______________________

2. If a person's life does not consist in the abundance of possessions, what does it consist of?

3. Which of the verses we studied speaks most clearly to your financial situation right now? What steps would you need to take to respond to this verse?

Copyright © 1995, The Standard Publishing Company. Permission to reproduce for ministry purposes only.

Dream Intruder #6

The Intruder of
Divorce

Divorce is ugly. Divorce turns married couples into courtroom opponents. It removes children from parents. It separates brothers from sisters. Many experts say divorce is harder to recover from than the death of a spouse because it's not final. The other party lives on. Your lives, though no longer joined by marriage, are joined by memories, families, children, and finances. And the scars last a lifetime. The pain defies description. This is why God wants marriage to be a lifelong commitment. He knows what is best. He isn't trying to be hard on us. He wants us to have the best possible life.

While churches have correctly stood for the sanctity of marriage, many have forgotten to balance their stand with the spirit of Christ, who specialized in accepting people nobody else would. Many divorced people want the grace of God, they want to know how God would have them move on in their lives, but so many churches keep them at arm's length, and they're left hurting, confused, in need of a touch from God.

God always starts with people where they are. God wants his family to be a community of "wounded healers." We help each other to rebuild broken lives and recover from dream intruders by the grace we ourselves have received.

—Adapted from *Dream Intruders,* by Gene Appel

Central Theme Though we must uphold the sanctity of marriage, we must also extend God's grace to people who have experienced divorce.

Lesson Aims Students will examine their own attitudes on divorce and divorced people, grasp the Bible's emphasis on both the importance of marriage and acceptance of people regardless of their sin or status, and identify practical ways to minister to divorced people.

Bible Background John 4:4–26; 2 Corinthians 5:16–19; Malachi 2:15, 16; Matthew 19:3–9

For Further Study Read Dream Intruder #6, "Divorce," in *Dream Intruders.*

PLAN ONE 

Classes

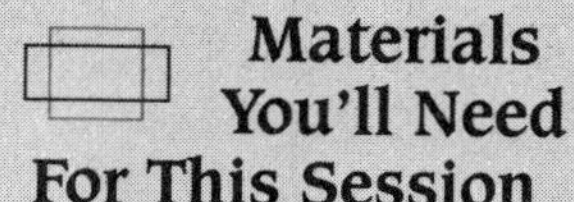

Materials You'll Need For This Session

Copies of all resource sheets, Transparency 6A, and pens or pencils

BUILDING COMMUNITY

Attitude Survey and Discussion
10 Minutes

Distribute copies of Resource Sheet 6A, "Divorce Attitude Survey," to the class. Ask participants to take a few minutes to respond privately to each of the statements. Encourage them not to take too long responding to any one statement, but simply to circle their gut-level reactions to each one. After a few minutes, ask them briefly to share in twos or threes with people sitting around them which statement they most strongly agreed with and which statement they most strongly disagreed with. (Remind the class that since divorce is a sensitive issue, we will need to treat others' views and attitudes with respect and sensitivity.)

OPTION
Group Sentence Completion
5–10 Minutes

Before students arrive, arrange chairs in several circles of six to eight, and write the word *DIVORCE* on the chalkboard or overhead so people will see it as they arrive. After everyone is seated in one of the circles, ask students to go around their circles and complete the following sentence: **The most difficult thing about divorce is . . .** (If your class is less than fifteen people, you could do this in one big circle.)

CONSIDERING SCRIPTURE

Make a transition to this section of the lesson: **Divorce is a difficult subject with much pain and disagreement attached to it. Today we will look at how God calls Christians to respond to divorce.** Then do one of the following Bible learning activities.

Group Bible Study and Report
20–25 Minutes

Show Transparency 6A, "The Church and the Divorced," and ask for examples of what the author is talking about: **How can a church keep divorced people at arm's length like this quote talks about? What examples of that can you think of?** After a few examples have been given, tell the class, **Today's Scripture will look both at the importance of marriage and the need for extending grace to people who have experienced divorce.**

Divide into three groups. Assign one group Resource Sheet 6B and distribute a copy to each person in the group. Do the same with Resource Sheet 6C for the second group and Resource Sheet 6D for the third group. Appoint a facilitator in each group. Have someone in each group read the Scripture listed on the sheet, and then the groups should answer the discussion questions that follow. Let the groups know they will need to have a representative report to the class on what they found after they are finished with their discussions.

After the groups have had time to complete their handouts, bring the class back together. Starting with the group that did sheet 6B, have the reporter read that group's Scripture out loud and share their conclusions with the class. Do the same with the groups that had sheets 6C and 6D. Have the reporter from the 6D group briefly paraphrase the story instead of reading the passage in its entirety.

Then move on to the next activity under "Reflecting and Responding."

Option

Lecture and Discussion

15–20 Minutes

Prepare a brief lecture and discussion incorporating the following material. (If the *Dream Intruders* handbook is available to you, you may also want to include information from the chapter on divorce.)

1. The commonness of divorce in our society

- One marriage dissolves every twenty-seven seconds.
- Thirty-nine percent of first marriages end in divorce.
- Sixty percent of second marriages end in divorce.
- Forty percent of the children born in the 1970s have spent part of their growing-up years in a single-parent household.

2. The pain of divorce for all involved

- A two-year "crazy period" starting after initial separation—spending sprees, drug and alcohol abuse, sexual promiscuity—is common.
- The emotional roller coaster: loneliness, guilt, low self-esteem.
- Effects on children: 73 percent decrease in standard of living; only 20 percent maintain good relationships with both parents; one in six sees his father only once a week; 52 percent haven't seen their dads in the last year.
- Rejection and estrangement from married friends, family, and sometimes church.

3. God's emphasis on both the sanctity of marriage and extending grace to the divorced person

- Jesus clearly said marriage is meant to be permanent: Matthew 19:6.
- Allowance for divorce is in extreme cases: Matthew 5:31, 32; 1 Corinthians 7:15.
- God says he hates divorce: Malachi 2:16.
- But God himself knows how divorced people feel: Jeremiah 3:8.
- Jesus' main concern with the woman at the well was her salvation, even though she'd had five husbands and was currently living with a man: John 4:4–26.

- We are called not to judge people based on worldly labels, but to see all people as God sees them: 2 Corinthians 5:16–19.

Show Transparency 6A, "The Church and the Divorced," and ask for examples of "keeping divorced people at arm's length." After a few examples are given, move on to the next activity.

Reflecting and Responding

Brainstorming
10 Minutes

Either in small groups or as a class, brainstorm ways that the church and individual Christians can minister to people who are experiencing the pain of divorce. You might want to ask the class to think in terms of how to respond during the two stages of the divorce process: the time between separation and divorce, and after the divorce. Write these ideas on an overhead or chalkboard. Be sure to call attention to things your church is already doing as well as looking for ways your church, your class, and individuals can begin ministering to divorcing and divorced people.

Option
Attitude Check
10–15 Minutes

Break into pairs or groups of three or four and discuss which attitudes from the survey in the "Building Community" activity were challenged by what was presented in class today. Discuss practical ways of overcoming these attitudes so that we can have more compassion for and outreach to divorced people.

PLAN TWO

Groups

BUILDING COMMUNITY

1. Where you grew up, what group of people was most looked down upon?

2. OPTION: Use one of the activities from "Building Community" in the Classes plan of this lesson.

CONSIDERING SCRIPTURE

Read the quote on the introductory page of this lesson. Then tell the group, **We will be looking at an encounter between Jesus and a woman in the first century who had a very common twentieth-century lifestyle: multiple marriages, multiple divorces, little respect for the sanctity of marriage.** Have someone read John 4:4–26 out loud. Then lead a discussion, selecting from the following questions.

1. What is the significance of the time and place of this conversation?
(Samaritans were people the Jews considered "half-breeds" and heretics. The sixth hour was high noon, when no one went out in the sun except people who were not welcome when everyone else was there during the better times of day.)

2. What do you think the Samaritan woman's tone was when she asked Jesus in verse 9, "How can you ask me for a drink?"

3. Why doesn't Jesus answer her question directly? (v.10)

4. What do you think Jesus intended by telling her to go get her husband? (v. 16)

5. Why did the woman turn the conversation into a religious controversy? (v. 19, 20)

6. What does it mean to worship God "in spirit and truth"? (v. 23)

Option

Accountability Partners

Suggest that accountability partners discuss what they have learned in this series about responding to things we cannot control. The following questions can be used to guide their discussion:

- Which dream intruder do you think would be the most difficult for you to handle? Which one do you think you would handle the best if it happened to you?

accidents ___
terminal illness ___
losing your job ___
bankruptcy ___
prodigal children ___
divorce ___

- What did you learn about yourself or your relationship with God when it comes to dealing with dream intruders?

- What do you need most to help you be prepared for the kinds of things we've discussed during this series?

Option

Memory Verse

"So from now on we regard no one from a worldly point of view. . . . God . . . reconciled us to himself through Christ and gave us the ministry of reconciliation" (2 Corinthians 5:16–18).

7. What seems to be Jesus' main concern throughout this conversation?

8. Why didn't Jesus say more to her about her many marriages and poor morals?

9. What do Jesus' actions and words in this story tell us about his attitude toward people who have fallen far short of upholding God's ideals and commandments on marriage?

Reflecting and Responding

Use some of the following questions either with the whole group or in smaller groups of three or four for more personal reflection and response.

1. Someone has said, "The church is the only army that shoots its wounded." How does the church or Christian individuals sometimes fall into the error of mistreating divorced people?

2. What attitudes about divorced people interfere with reaching out to them?

3. How can we go about maintaining respect for the sanctity of marriage without mistreating people who have gone through or are going through divorce?

4. Is the best way to minister to divorced people to give them their own classes and groups? Why or why not?

5. Do you find it easier to accept someone who was the so-called "innocent party" in a divorce?

6. What are some practical ways the church can minister to divorced people?

7. How can we as individual Christians minister to divorced people?

Divorce Attitude Survey

Read the following attitudes. Circle a response after each statement to indicate how much it matches your thoughts and feelings on the issue of divorce. (Be as honest as you can!)

1. It's acceptable to get divorced as long as you weren't the one who ended the marriage.

Strongly Agree Agree Unsure Disagree Strongly Disagree

2. Divorce should be looked down upon by society, as it used to be, so people wouldn't be so quick to get divorced.

Strongly Agree Agree Unsure Disagree Strongly Disagree

3. As long as the grounds for divorce are scriptural, I don't have a problem with it.

Strongly Agree Agree Unsure Disagree Strongly Disagree

4. Divorce is often a sign of personal weakness or failure.

Strongly Agree Agree Unsure Disagree Strongly Disagree

5. Divorce could happen to anyone.

Strongly Agree Agree Unsure Disagree Strongly Disagree

6. Most people who get divorced don't try hard enough to work out their problems.

Strongly Agree Agree Unsure Disagree Strongly Disagree

7. If children are not involved, divorce isn't so bad.

Strongly Agree Agree Unsure Disagree Strongly Disagree

8. There shouldn't be "no fault" divorce in the courts; it's always someone's fault.

Strongly Agree Agree Unsure Disagree Strongly Disagree

9. It is better to get divorced than to endure a lifeless or unfulfilling relationship.

Strongly Agree Agree Unsure Disagree Strongly Disagree

10. If a friend of mine got divorced, no matter what the circumstances, it wouldn't significantly change our relationship.

Strongly Agree Agree Unsure Disagree Strongly Disagree

11. The best thing a church can do for divorced people is to give them their own group or class so they can be with other divorced people.

Strongly Agree Agree Unsure Disagree Strongly Disagree

12. If both parties truly want the divorce, that makes their divorce acceptable.

Strongly Agree Agree Unsure Disagree Strongly Disagree

Copyright © 1995, The Standard Publishing Company. Permission to reproduce for ministry purposes only.

Bible Study Group #1

Read the following Scriptures, and then answer the questions that follow.
Be prepared to give a report to the class of your main findings from this exercise.

MALACHI 2:15, 16

1. Why does God bring up the subject of divorce here? What is the context?

2. What does the context of this verse tell us about why God hates divorce?

3. Is it possible to be guilty of unfaithfulness to your spouse without getting divorced or committing adultery?

4. Do you think God looks at cold, unloving marriages the same way he looks at divorce? Why or why not?

MATTHEW 19:3–9

1. Why does Jesus respond to the question about the lawfulness of divorce by talking about the oneness of marriage instead of simply saying whether or not it is acceptable to divorce?

2. Does the allowance of divorce because of adultery mean that someone should divorce if a spouse is unfaithful?

Questions for Consideration

1. How can we teach these two passages wholeheartedly without becoming legalistic and judgmental of people who have not obeyed them?

2. On what basis should someone decide to divorce or not divorce if his or her spouse has committed adultery?

Copyright © 1995, The Standard Publishing Company. Permission to reproduce for ministry purposes only.

Bible Study Group #2

Read the following Scripture, and then answer the questions that follow.
Be prepared to give a report to the class of your main findings from this exercise.

2 Corinthians 5:16–19

1. What does it mean to regard someone from a "worldly point of view" (NIV)?

2. What would it mean for us as Christians to regard a divorced person from a worldly point of view?

3. Can someone be a new creature in Christ if he divorced for unscriptural reasons and does not seem repentant or remorseful? Why or why not?

4. What does it mean that Christ "gave us this ministry of reconciliation"?

Copyright © 1995, The Standard Publishing Company. Permission to reproduce for ministry purposes only.

Bible Study Group #3

Read the following Scripture, and then answer the questions that follow.
Be prepared to give a report to the class of your main findings from this exercise.

JOHN 4:4–26

1. What do you think Jesus intended by telling the woman to go get her husband?

2. Why didn't Jesus say more to her about her many marriages and poor morals?

3. What seems to be Jesus' main concern throughout this conversation?

4. What do Jesus' actions and words in this story tell us about his attitude toward people who have fallen far short of upholding God's ideals and commandments on marriage?

Copyright © 1995, The Standard Publishing Company. Permission to reproduce for ministry purposes only.

"While churches have correctly stood
for the sanctity of marriage,
many have forgotten to balance their stand
with the spirit of Christ, who specialized
in accepting people nobody else would.
Many divorced people want the grace of God,
they want to know how God
would have them move on in their lives,
but so many churches
keep them at an arm's length,
and they're left hurting, confused,
in need of a touch from God."

—Adapted from *Dream Intruders,* by Gene Appel

Copyright © 1995, The Standard Publishing Company. Permission to reproduce for ministry purposes only.

OTHER *CREATIVE GROUPS GUIDES*
from Standard Publishing

A CALL TO PRAYER

Guide by Jan Johnson
Learn to pray more effectively, more sincerely, with more power, and without hindrances. Class or group members will gain practical knowledge about why they should pray, how to pray, and what to pray for. Start a prayer revival in your congregation!
Order number 11-40309 *(ISBN 0-7847-0309-4)*

CLAIMING YOUR PLACE

Guide by Michael C. Mack and Mark A. Taylor
Help your small group or class learn how to find where they fit into the life of the church. Seven sessions will guide your group to greater commitment and involvement in the body. They'll find a place of faith, service, bold witness, passion, and more.
Order number 11-40305 *(ISBN 0-7847-0285-3)*

HEARING GOD

Guide by Michael C. Mack and Mark A. Taylor
Help your group or class learn how to read God's Word—and really understand it! In just six lessons, you will demonstrate eight simple steps that can make anyone feel at home in the Bible and be able to put it into practice.
Order number 11-40306 *(ISBN 0-7847-0286-1)*

FIND US FAITHFUL

Guide by Michael D. McCann
Help your group members learn to pass on their faith to the next generation, to their children, and to others in their spheres of influence. Christianity is always one generation from extinction, so it is critical that we learn how to pass on our faith.
Order number 11-40308 *(ISBN 0-7847-0308-6)*

To order, contact your local Christian bookstore.
(If the book is out of stock, you can order by calling 1-800-543-1353.)

To purchase a copy of
Dream Intruders,
contact your local
Christian bookstore.

(If the book is out of stock, you can order by calling 1-800-543-1353.)

11-40301 *(ISBN 0-7847-0051-6)*